All Rights Reserved © 2023

SCHEDULE

FRIDAY, MARCH 3rd

5:30pm   Check-In

5:45pm   Dinner

6:30pm   Welcome, Announcements, Ice-Breaker

7:00pm   Worship through Song

7:15pm   Session 1

8:00pm   Dessert & Coffee

8:15pm   Door Prize/Small Group Discussion

9:00pm   Dismissal & Optional Late Night Chat

SATURDAY, MARCH 4ᵀᴴ

8:30pm Check-In/Door Prizes

8:45pm Worship through Song

9:00am Session 2

9:40am Break/Snacks

9:50am Breakout Session 1

10:50am Break/Snacks

11:00am Breakout Session 2

12:00pm Lunch/Door Prizes

12:20pm Small Group Discussion

12:40pm Session 3

1:20pm Feedback Forms

1:30pm Dismissal

KEYNOTE SPEAKER BIO

Patty Den Hartog

Patty has been married to Don for 45 years and they have lived in a number of different states as the Lord directed Don in full-time ministry. Their first year of marriage was in Omaha, then they moved to Dallas, Texas, while Don attended Dallas seminary. After graduation he was a youth pastor in Iowa, then they moved to Kansas for his first pastorate. From there they moved back to Iowa, then North Dakota, and then Virginia. They lived in Virginia for 17 years before moving to Kansas a little over a year ago.

Don and Patty have four children. Their oldest is Christy, married to Jason, and they have three children. Next is Brian, married to Kimbra, and they have seven. Karen, married to Dan, have three. Brad, married to Valerie, have two children. Don and Patty also have three little ones waiting for the in the kingdom.

A passion of Patty's is being a grandma. She has made many flights between Virginia and Nebraska/Kansas. Another passion she has is working with young moms. She would also consider supporting her husband in his ministry a passion, as she is passionate about him teaching the Bible and what he teaches. Some of the top fun things she enjoys doing is going on bike rides, reading, and exploring new places.

SESSION 1 NOTES

SESSION 2 NOTES

BREAKOUT SESSION 1 OPTIONS

Parenting: What do we desire for our kids and How do we get there? The Scripture as our Guide.
By Lori Bolerjack Room 125

Lori has been married to Brent for 15 years and they have three children- Millie (14), Greta (12), and George (10). Lori spends her days homeschooling her kids and managing the home and family schedule. She is passionate about growing in the truths of God's Word, cultivating healthy marriages, hearing about the Lord's work around the world and teaching/training her kids to know and love Jesus. For fun, Lori likes spending time with her family and friends, date nights with Brent, playing games, going for walks with her kids, and being outdoors.

In this breakout we are going to look at WHAT we really desire for our children, and how that compares with what the world and the Bible tell us we should value. Today, there are an abundance of philosophies and opinions on what we should do as parents and how we should do it. How can we discern the good and bad of those ideas? Do they line up with the wisdom of God's Word? We will also look at practical ways of HOW to raise our children in light of God's parenting principles.

Women at the Well
by Christie Funderburk- Room 111

Christie grew up near Houston, Texas, and came to know about Jesus through a Bible church where her dad was the pastor. She met her husband, Scott, at Texas Tech. They have been married for 29 years and have two children, Drew (20) and Grace (20) whom they adopted from Russia as infants. For fun, Christie loves the outdoors, including hiking and swimming, playing the keyboard, music and playing games with friends and family. She is passionate about encouraging Christians to do life together and inviting others to join the journey.

This breakout session is designed to explore how we can be intentional about enhancing and strengthening the relationships we already have, and building new ones that can bring hope and encouragement to each other for the glory of God. So, let's "Gather at the Well" and discover that our true thirst for fellowship can be satisfied together in Christ.

BREAKOUT SESSION 1 NOTES

BREAKOUT SESSION 2 OPTIONS

Fellowship of the Ring: A Husband's Perspective on Life Together
by Kamie Barrick   Room 111

Kamie Barrick has been married to Lance for almost 15 years. They have three beautiful children, Scout (11), Smith (7), and Eleanor (4). She enjoys the small things of life including her 12 chickens, classical literature, preparing warm meals, and working in her garden as well as a good DIY project. She has been blessed by many 'ladies of wisdom' throughout her life who continue to help refine her as a wife and mother.

Oftentimes women can be heard describing our significant others as "Mr. Fix-It", workaholics, always ready to fight, hard-headed, prince charming, the knight in shining armor, etc. These descriptions, although founded on the sincerity of a woman's heart, do not fully depict God's design of man. Consequently, this leads to strained fellowship between us and our husbands. This session will explore how these descriptions can be found in scripture as attributes of man, made in the image of God. When we properly understand these attributes, we can anticipate the fruitfulness that comes from cohesive fellowship with our husbands.

Even Though . . . It is Well; The Four R's of Trusting God in Hard Times
by Nicole Stauffer Room 125

Nicole Stauffer is a homeschool mom of 10 children. All but one are still living at home. She and her husband, DJ, have been married for 30 wonderful years. Their children, Grace -25, Sarah - 23, Noah-22, Daniel and Stephen (twins) - 21, Simeon - 17, Hope - 16, Esther - 15, Faith - 12, and John - 8 are her greatest blessings. Nicole's passions are the free grace message and being a mom. She enjoys sharing great books with her kids, playing Catan and Dominion and other games, as well as playing ping pong. Reading a little each evening is her favorite way to unwind, and her hobbies also include scrapbooking and sewing when she can find the time.

Children's health problems, losing a parent, miscarriage, losing a brother, and being without a church for 5 years are just a few of the trials that I have experienced in the past 30 years of marriage. God uses hard times to help us grow and mature. But often, when hard times come, we forget all about that and just fall apart or get angry. And sometimes we feel alone or forgotten. I would like to share my story with you and the passages and principles that have helped and continue to help me as hard times come. Hopefully you will come away encouraged and ready to face whatever comes your way and be able to say, "Even though . . . it IS well with my soul."

Quiet Time-
Personal Time With Jesus
by Lois Fisher Room 105

Lois loves to strengthen her walk with Jesus, study God's word and help other to strengthen their fellowship with Christ. She moved to Stillwater in 2015 to be near her grandson and his parents. She is a retired educator after serving public schools as teacher and administrator for 54 years. Her favorite things to do
are spending time with family and friends, antique shopping, and traveling.

Quiet time is a time set aside in a certain place where a person can get away, be alone and draw near to the Lord. In this session, information will be provided to assist in planning and preparing for this important time of the day, to make this a consistent time, and how to gain the benefits of praying and listening to God by
reading His Word. ...He rewards those who earnestly seek Him Hebrews 11:6b

BREAKOUT SESSION 2 NOTES

SESSION 3 NOTES

Made in the USA
Columbia, SC
13 February 2023